Literary Venice

Laurence Hutton

Alpha Editions

This edition published in 2022

ISBN : 9789356890916

Design and Setting By
Alpha Editions
www.alphaedis.com
Email - info@alphaedis.com

INTRODUCTION

IN a chapter upon "Literary Residences," among *The Curiosities of Literature*, Isaac D'Israeli said: "No foreigners, men of letters, lovers of the arts, or even princes, would pass through Antwerp without visiting the House of Rubens, to witness the animated residence of genius, and the great man who conceived the idea." This volume is intended to be a record of the Animated Residences of Genius which are still existing in Venice; and it is written for the foreigners, for the Men of Letters, for the lovers of art, and even for the princes who pass through the town, and who care to make such houses a visit.

It is the result of many weeks of patient but pleasant study of Venice itself. Everything here set down has been verified by personal observation, and is based upon the reading of scores of works of travel and biography. It is the Venice I know in the real life of the present and in the literature of the past; and to me it is Venice from its best and most interesting side.

The Queen of the Adriatic is peculiarly poor in local guide-books and in local maps. In the former are to be found but slight reference to that part of Venice which is most dear to the lovers of bookmen and to the lovers of books; and the latter contain the names of none but the larger of the squares, streets, and canals, leaving, in many instances, the searcher after the smaller thoroughfares entirely afloat in the Adriatic, with no compass by which to steer.

The stranger in Venice, accustomed to the nomenclature of the streets and the avenues, the alleys and the courts, of the cities and towns with which he is familiar in other parts of the world, may be interested to learn that here a large canal is called a *Rio*, or a *Canale*; that a *Calle* is a street open at both ends; that a *Rio Terrà* is a street which was once a canal; that a *Ramo* is a small, narrow street, branching out of a larger one; that a *Salizzada* is a wide, paved street; that a *Ruga* is just a street; that a *Rughetta*, or a *Piscina*, is a little street; that a *Riva* is a narrow footway along the bank of a canal; that a *Fondamenta* is a longer and a broader passage-way, a quay, or an embankment; that a *Corte* is a court-yard; that a *Sottoportico* is an entrance into a court, through, or under, a house—that which in Edinburgh is called a *Pend*, and in Paris a *Cité*; that a large square is a *Piazza*; that a small square is a *Piazzetta*, or a *Campo*; that a small campo is a *Campiello*; that a plain, commonplace house is a *Casa*; that a mansion is a *Palazzo*; that an island is an *Isola*; that a bridge is a *Ponte*; that a tower is a *Campanile*; that a ferry is a *Traghetto*; that a parish is a *Parrochia*; and that a district is a *Contrada*, or a *Sistiere*.

Armed with this information, the readers must do the rest for themselves.

To Mrs. Clara Erskine Clement, to Miss Henrietta Macy, to Mrs. Walter F. Brown, to Mr. Charles Dudley Warner, to Dr. Alexander Robertson, to Mr. William Logsdail, I owe my thanks for much valuable information given me while I was enlarging, elaborating, and revising the article, printed in *Harper's Magazine* for July, 1896, upon which this volume is based.

LAURENCE HUTTON.

Casa Frolo,
50 Giudecca.

LITERARY LANDMARKS OF VENICE

IT is almost impossible for any one who is at all familiar with the voluminous amount of literature relating to the history and to the art of Venice, to refrain from quoting, voluntarily or involuntarily, what he has read and absorbed concerning "the dangerous and sweet-charmed town," which Ruskin calls a golden city paved with emerald, and which Goethe said is a city which can only be compared with itself. Comparisons in Venice are certainly as odorous as are some of its canals, while many of its streets are not only paved with emerald, but are frescoed now with glaring End-of-the-Nineteenth-Century advertisements of dentifrice and sewing-machines.

That which first strikes the observant stranger in Venice, to-day, is the fact that the Venetians have absolutely and entirely lost their grip upon the beautiful. Nothing on earth can be finer than the art of its glory; nothing in the world can be viler than the so-called art of its decadence. That the descendants of the men who decorated the palaces of five or six hundred years ago could have conceived, or endured, the wall-papers, the stair-carpets, and the hat-racks in the Venetian hotels of the present, is beyond belief. Whatever is old is magnificent, from the madonnas of Gian Bellini to the window of the Cicogna Palace on the Fondamenta Briati. Whatever is new is ugly, from the railway-station at one end of the Grand Canal to the gas-house at the other. And the iron bridges, and the steamboats, and the drop-curtain in the Malibran Theatre are the worst of all.

When the English-speaking and the English-reading visitors in Venice, for whom this volume is written, overcome the feeling that they are predestined to fall into one of the canals before they leave the city; when they become accustomed to being driven about in a hearse-shaped, one-manned row-boat; when they have been shown all the traditional sights, have bought the regulation old brass and old glass, have learned to draw smoke out of the long, thin, black, rat-tailed straw-covering things the Venetians call cigars—when they have seen and have done all these, they will find themselves much more interested in the house in which Byron lived, and in the perfectly restored palace in which Browning died, than in the half-ruined, wholly decayed mansions of all the Doges who were ever Lord Mayors of Venice. The guide-books tell us where Faliero plotted and where Foscari fell, where Desdemona suffered and where Shylock traded; but they give us no hint as to where Sir Walter Scott lodged or where Rogers breakfasted, or what was done here by the many English-speaking Men of Letters who have made Venice known to us, and properly understood. Upon these chiefly it is my purpose here to dwell.

Venice, with all her literature, has brought forth but few literary men of her own. There are but few poets among her legitimate sons, and few were the poets she adopted. The early annalists and the later historians were almost the only writers of importance who were entitled to call her mother; and to most of these she has been, though kindly, little more than a step-mother or a mother-in-law.

Shakspere, who wrote much about Venice, and who probably never saw it, remarked once that all the world's a stage. Venice, even now, is a grand spectacular show; and no drama ever written is more dramatic than is Venice itself. Mr. Howells prefaces his *Venetian Life* by an account of the play, and the by-play, which he once saw from a stage-box in the little theatre in Padua, when the prompters, and the scene-shifters, and the actors in the wings, were as prominent to him as were the tragedians and comedians who strutted, and mouthed, and sawed the air with their hands, in full view of the house; and he adds: "It has sometimes seemed to me as if fortune had given me a stage-box at another and grander spectacle, and that I had been suffered to see this Venice, which is to other cities like the pleasant improbability of the theatre to everyday, commonplace life, to much the same effect as that melodrama in Padua." It has been my own good fortune to spend, at various seasons, a short time in the pit—"on a standee ticket"—just to drop in for a moment now and then, when the performance is nearly over, and to look not so much at the broken-down stage and its worn-out settings, not so much at the actors and at the acting, as to study the audiences, the crowds of men and women in parquet, gallery, and boxes, who have been sitting for centuries through the different thrilling acts of the great plays played here; and have applauded, or hissed, as the case may be.

So strange and so strong is the power of fiction over truth, in Venice, as everywhere else, that Portia and Emilia, Cassio, Antonio, and Iago, appear to have been more real here than are the women and men of real life. We see, on the Rialto, Shylock first, and then its history and its associations; and the Council Chamber of the Palace of the Doges is chiefly interesting as being the scene of Othello's eloquent defence of himself.

It is a curious fact, recorded by Th. Elze, and quoted by Mr. Horace Howard Furness, in his Appendix to *The Merchant of Venice*, that at the time of the action of that drama, in Shakspere's own day, there was living in Padua a professor of the University whose characteristics fully and entirely corresponded with all the qualities of "Old Bellario," and with all the requisites of the play. In his concluding passages Elze described the University of Padua at the close of the Sixteenth Century, when there were representatives of twenty-three nations among its students. He said that not a few Englishmen took up their abode in Padua, for a longer or a shorter time, for the purposes of study; all of whom must naturally have visited Venice. "And," he added, "if it has been hitherto impossible to prove that Shakspere drew his knowledge of Venice and Padua, and the region about, from personal observation, it is quite possible to suppose that he obtained it by word of mouth, either from Italians living in England,

THE COUNCIL-CHAMBER OF THE DOGES. IN OTHELLO'S TIME

or from Englishmen who had pursued their studies at Padua."

Among the significant names given by Elze as students at Padua are Rosenkranz, in 1587 to 1589, and Guldenstern, in 1603.

One of the most distinguished of the English representatives who took up his abode in Padua in the middle of the Eighteenth Century, was Oliver Goldsmith, who, according to John Forster, received his degree there, although there is no official record of such a fact.

Signor Giuseppe Tassini, in his *Curiosità Veneziane*, published in 1863, gives the following account of what is known as "Othello's House," which has, in all probability, never before been put into English, and is here roughly translated. At the right-hand side of the Campo del Carmine, or on the little canal of the same name, he says, in effect, stands what is left of an ancient palace supposed, but incorrectly, to have belonged once to an influential family called Moro. Christoforo Moro, a cadet of the house, was sent to Cyprus in 1505; and he returned in 1508 to relate to the magnificos of his native city his adventures there, having in the meantime lost his first wife. In 1515 he was married again, and to Demonia Bianco, daughter of Donato da Lazze. Rawdon Brown and other writers, continues Signor Tassini, believe that upon this hint Shakspere spoke, making Othello a Moor, as a play upon the name Moro, and turning Demonia Bianco into Desdemona. But he adds that the Goro, not the Moro, family lived here in the beginning of the Sixteenth Century, the latter occupying a palace in the Campo di S. Giovanni Decollato, now the Campo S. Zan Degolà, some distance away.

Confusing the names of Goro and Moro, and fancying that the ancient figure of a warrior standing on the corner of the Campo del Carmine house, now blackened by time, although not so black as he is painted, represents a Moor, the guides and the gondoliers, and even the antiquaries, of Venice have given to "Othello's House," according to Signor Tassini, a local reputation and a name which it does not merit.

The beautiful little Gothic Palazzo Contarini-Fasan, built in the Fourteenth Century and done over at the end of the Nineteenth, on the right bank of the Grand Canal, going towards the Rialto, and near the Grand Hotel, seems to have no excuse, either from tradition or from any confusion of names, for calling itself "the House of Desdemona" at all. Its only dramatic interest to-day consists in the fact that it has been the home of Signora Eleonora Duse, the leading actress of Italy, who is called by her admirers the Italian Sara Bernhardt, although she has genius enough of her own to warrant her being compared with no one but herself.

And thus perish, at the hands of a transatlantic, present-day iconoclast and grubber after the truth, two of the most cherished of the Landmarks of Venice.

Mr. Hare is of the opinion that the Doge Christoforo Moro, buried in the Church of S. Giobbe in the Canareggio District, is the Moro of the Othello legend, although he died in 1470, almost half a century before Signor Tassini married him to Desdemona; and his tomb, in the chancel of the church, as Mr. Hare points out, "is ornamented with the moro or mulberry, which was his family device." It will be remembered that Othello inherited from his mamma a handkerchief spotted with strawberries (mulberries?) which played an important part in the great tragedy of his life.

Christoforo Moro lies under a large flat stone in front of the altar of the church. The slab has been greatly defaced by the tread of generations of priests and of acolytes, but its carvings still bear distinct traces of fruits which to-day look as much like strawberries as mulberries, while certain of their leaves are decidedly of the strawberry form. A portrait of Doge Moro hangs in the sacristy of S. Giobbe. It exhibits a face in which there are no signs of the duskiness which dramatic tradition has given to Othello during all these years, but which is hard enough to have silenced the most dreadful belle who ever frighted the isle from its propriety.

Mr. Hare also explains that a story very like to that of Shakspere's *Othello* was told

THE OTHELLO HOUSE

in the seventh novella of the third decade of Giovanni Battista Cinthio's collection of stories, called the *Ecatomiti*, in which the name of the heroine is the same, and in which the original Iago suggested to Othello that a stocking filled with sand might be an admirable weapon against his wife if it were judiciously applied to her back. Mr. Hare quotes Bishop Bollani as writing in 1602, June 1st: "The day before yesterday, a Sanudo, living in the Rio della Croce, on the Giudecca, compelled his wife, a lady of the Cappello family, to go to confession, and the following night, towards the fifth hour, plunged a dagger into her heart and killed her. It is said that she had been unfaithful to him, but the voice of her neighborhood proclaimed her a saint."

The voice of the gallery has proclaimed Desdemona a saint ever since!

The Venetians still believe implicitly in the statue of the sunburnt warrior, and in Shakspere's history of his life. And Mr. Howells's gondolier not only showed him the house of Cassio, near the Rialto Bridge, but was ready to point out the residence of the amiable Iago and of Emilia, his wife. Cassio, I may remark, is said here to have been Desdemona's cousin, and Iago is believed to have been the major-domo of the distracted household.

The modern Venetian dealers in second-hand portraits, and the venders of bric-à-brac of all kinds, seem to have learned their strict and universal Economy of Truth from the memorial tablets over their shops. If you are offered here an article of original, homemade, present-time antiquity for five lire, you may depend upon getting it for two lire and a half, and you may be sure that it costs you, even then, about twice as much as it is worth. If an inscription in old Latin or in choice Italian tells you that "Here lived" some particular Venetian hero of sword or pen, you may put down in your diary that he probably visited next door, or that he died over the way.

The tablet devoted to Marco Polo, however, being upon the side of a play-house where fiction is supposed to reign supreme, seems to have established itself as the exception which proves this rule. Only a small portion of the Palazzo dei Polo now remains. What is left of it is little more than a fragment of an outside staircase in a corner of the Corte Millione in the Canareggio District. The mansion at one time covered no small part of the neighboring territory, which still bears distinct traces of wealthy and aristocratic occupancy. Over the door-way of the Malibran Theatre, on the Rio del Teatro Malibran, is an inscription stating that "This was the house of Marco Polo, who travelled in the remotest parts of Asia, and described them. This tablet was placed here by the Commune in 1881."

The great voyager was born in this house, and here he spent, in comparative quiet, after many years of toilsome but profitable travel, the last days of his life. Having, like Shakspere's banish'd Norfolk, retired himself to Italy, here in Venice he gave his body to this pleasant country's earth, in 1323 or thereabouts. How far the rest of the quotation is applicable to his peculiar case no man, of course, can say. Polo was called by alliterative neighbors "Mark the Millionaire"—hence the "Corte Millione"; and the rich man, proverbially, does not find heaven a place of easy access.

The Corte Millione, Polo's court-yard, is now the *al-fresco* foyer of the Malibran Theatre, which was built originally in 1678. But hardly one of the millions of Venetian youths who, for more than two centuries, have cooled themselves under the stars, by the side of Polo's old well and Polo's old marble balustrade, between the acts of the play or the ballet, ever heard of Mark the Millionaire, or care where he lived or where he died.

The mystery as to the exact part of this pleasant country's earth which received Marco Polo's body has never been cleared up. In a copy of his last will and testament, I read, however, that he left a certain sum of money to the Monastery of Saint Lawrence here, "where I desire to be buried." He certainly buried his father, Nicolò Polo, in the old and original Church of S. Lorenzo; and the natural inference is that he himself lies somewhere within its precincts. The sarcophagus erected for the elder Polo by the filial care of the younger Polo is known to have existed, until towards the end of the Sixteenth Century, in the porch leading to the church.

The old building was renewed, from its very foundations, in 1592, and no traces of the ancient structure remain; the old parochial records no longer exist, and even the name of the Polos is as unknown to the parochial authorities to-day as it is to the worldlings who crowd the theatre erected upon the site of the house which was their home.

Petrarch is known to have made several visits to Venice, and he is said to have been very familiar with it, and very fond of it, even in his youth. In 1353 or '54 he was certainly here, for a short time, in an official capacity; and documentary evidence clearly proves that he settled in Venice in 1362—a cholera year—and remained here until 1368, making annual excursions to Padua, and spending certain of the summer and autumn months with friends at Pavia. During this

DEL PETRARCHA. E. DI M. LAVRA.

period he determined to bequeath a portion of his rich library to Venice for the use of students and the general public, and as an example to other men. He was highly esteemed by the Venetians, and his house was the meeting-place of the wise and the powerful. Boccaccio was his guest here for many months; they talked and walked, and they sailed the canals and the lagoons together in perfect sympathy; and there still exists a letter of Petrarch to Boccaccio, asking the latter poet to come again, and to stay longer next time.

Signor N. Barozzi, in a volume entitled *Petrarca e Venezia*, published in Venice in 1874, reprints, from the old plan of the city, now in the Archæological Museum, a rough sketch of Petrarch's house during his residence here between 1362 and 1368; and he seems to establish the fact that it was hired by the poet, not presented to him by the city, as is generally believed. It was then called the Palazzo del Molin, and it stood near to the Ponte del Sepolcro on the Riva degli Schiavoni, a broad promenade and wharf a short distance east of the Ducal Palace. This house, according to Petrarch himself, was humble enough; it had two towers, a style of architecture not uncommon in those days; and according to Signor Barozzi it was, later, a monastery, and at the present time is occupied as a barrack. If Signor Barozzi and the plan are correct, it is *not* the house marked by the tablet, and pointed out in the guide-books as Petrarch's, but the building on the corner of the little Calle del Dose, and some forty or fifty paces to the east of the generally accepted spot.

The two original towers of the Petrarch house disappeared long ago; the entire front is new and ugly, and the rear portions, although they are old and picturesque, do not date back to the Fourteenth Century. There is, probably, no part of the mansion left, as Petrarch knew and loved it, except, perhaps, the pavement of the court-yard. Even the old marble well is not as old as the days of the great poet. The interior of the establishment is not now seen of the public, except by permission of the military authorities, but it is one of the most interesting of the Landmarks of Venice, because of its association with the two immortal men who once adorned it.

Petrarch from his tower had a perfect view of the city and of the Adriatic, watching as he did the navies of the then known world as they entered and left the harbor, and looking out over the sea and down upon the crowds of busy men. His life here was, no doubt, a happy one; as must be the life of any man who brings to Venice some knowledge of its history, some idea of its art, some fondness for its traditions, and letters of introduction to some of its men of mind in all professions.

Signor Tassini says that while Petrarch lived here he often enjoyed the society of his natural daughter, Francesca, who once, in this house, and in the absence of her father, received the sad news of the death, at her home in Pavia, of her infant child; when Boccaccio acted as comforter, and tried in vain to stay her maternal tears.

Mr. Horatio F. Brown and Mr. Howells both quote a letter, written in Latin, by Petrarch to his friend Pietro Bolognese, in which he describes a famous festival held in the Piazza S. Marco to celebrate a victory over the Greeks in Candia. The poet was seated in the place of honor, at the right of the Doge, in the gallery of the Cathedral, and in front of the bronze horses;

and he tells of the many youths, decked in purple and gold, ruling with the rein, and urging with the spur, their horses in the then unpaved square, and watched by a throng of spectators so great that a grain of barley could not have fallen to the ground. There is not a horse in all Venice to-day; the youths wear ulsters when it is cold, and very little of anything when it is hot; and every grain of barley which falls to the ground is ravenously devoured by the doves, who alone of all the Venetians wear the purple now. If tradition, for the once, speaks truly, these very doves are the direct descendants of the carrier-pigeons which brought to Admiral Dandolo information from spies in Candia leading to the capture of the island, and which may have received grains of barley from the hand of Petrarch himself. As such do the doves of the present day receive grains of barley from me.

Mr. Brown, in his admirable study of *The Venetian Printing Press*, says that Aldus is not known, of a certainty, to have lived in the house, or even on the site of the house, No. 2311 Rio Terra Secondo, in the parish of S. Agostino, which is marked with a tablet

THE HOUSE OF PETRARCH

as his. But the fact that there still exists a letter addressed to Gregoropoulos at the little narrow Calle del Pistor, close by, and written while Gregoropoulos was employed by Aldus as corrector of Greek manuscript and Greek proof, would seem to imply that the famous printing-press may have stood in the latter street, if such a gutter can be called a street at all. It resembles no thoroughfares elsewhere in the world except the closes of Edinburgh; but it is not unlikely to have been the scene of the birth of the Aldines so dearly prized by the bookworms of to-day. The original Aldus is believed to have settled in Venice about 1488. As Mrs. Clara Erskine

Clement remarks, he was no mere printer; and although it is by that name now that he is most frequently regarded, he was a scholar before he was a printer, and he became a printer because of his scholarship. Concerning the many troublesome visitors to his place of business who went there to gossip and to kill their time, Aldus wrote, upon a later establishment: "We make bold to admonish such, in classical words, in a sort of edict placed over our door, 'Whoever you are, Aldo requests you, if you want anything ask for it in a few words and depart, unless, like Hercules, you come to lend the aid of your shoulders to the weary Atlas. Here will always be found, in that case, something for you to do, however many you may be.'"

Aldo Pio transferred the business in, or about, 1506 to the Campo S. Paternian, now called the Campo Manin; and there he lived and printed good books and good literature, succeeded by his son and his grandson. A very modern Bank for Savings now occupies the site of this establishment, and covers the entire back of the square. But a marble tablet of recent date, placed on its side, bears an inscription to the effect that "Aldo Pio, Paolo, and Aldo II., Manuzio, Princes in the Art of Typography in the Sixteenth Century, diffused, with classic books from this place, a new light of cultured wisdom"; the translation being by Dr. Alexander Robertson. This Campo S. Paternian house was probably that which bore the inscription quoted above, and relating to Atlas and the intellectual Hercules.

According to tradition, a certain Hercules named Erasmus came, in 1506, to lend his shoulder to the support of the load; and found something to do. Erasmus in the workshop of Aldus, printing, perhaps, his own *Adages*, is a picture for a poet or a painter to conjure with. Venice in all its glory never saw a greater sight.

Luther is known to have passed through Venice a few years later than this. He is supposed to have lodged in the cloisters of the Church of S. Stefano here, on his way to Rome, and to have celebrated mass at its high altar. S. Stefano is near the square of the same name, and it is not otherwise particularly distinguished. It dates back to the end of the Thirteenth and the beginning of the Fourteenth Century.

Another Hercules, as great in his way as was Erasmus, lent the aid of his shoulders to the weary Atlas of the Aldine Press in the Sixteenth Century; to wit, Paolo Sarpi, Scholar, Scientist, Philosopher, Statesman, Author, and Martyr, whom Gibbon called "the incomparable historian of the Council of Trent," and who is called by his present-day biographer, Dr. Robertson, "the greatest of Venetians."

Sarpi was born in Venice, in 1552; he was educated in Venice; in Venice he spent the better part of his life; in Venice he died; and in Venice he was very much buried. He was brutally stabbed by hired assassins while crossing the Ponte dei Pugni, in 1607; but he recovered, and did not surrender his indomitable soul until 1623.

Sarpi's posthumous fate for two centuries was an exceedingly restless one. His body was interred originally at the foot of an altar in the Servite Church here, with which he was intimately associated. In 1624 the Servite friars, warned of an intended desecration of his grave, removed his bones to a secret place in their monastery. The next year they carried them back to the church. In 1722 they were removed to still another part of the same church. In 1828, the whole establishment having become a ruin, Sarpi's bones were carried to the Seminary belonging to, and adjoining, S. Maria della Salute. They were next transferred to a private house in the parish of S. Biagio; then they were kept, for a time, in the Library of Saint Mark, in the Doge's Palace, and finally they were placed under a slab, near the main entrance of the Church of S. Michele, on the Cemetery Island of that name, where, after having been once more disturbed, in 1846, it is to be hoped they will be permitted to rest.

The church of the Servites no longer exists. A fragment of its ancient wall and two fine old door-ways, however, are still left. The main entrance, long ago bricked up, remains to-day, with one other old gate, which was the entrance to the monastery; and that is all. The larger portion of the site of the foundation is a flower garden; a modern chapel, dedicated in 1894, occupies a small corner of the ground. And the rest is an industrial school for poor girls, from seven to twenty-one years of age, who here, without cost to themselves, are educated for a self-supporting, useful life; as noble a monument as Paolo Sarpi could wish or have. The remains of the church of the Servites may be reached by the Rio di S. Fosca; and they stand in the parish of S. Maria dell' Orto. Here Sarpi wrote his almost countless works, from a *Treatise on the Interdict*, and a *History of Ecclesiastical Benefices*, to the *History of the Uscocks*, a band of pirates who infested the Dalmatian coast.

An elaborate statue of Sarpi, erected in 1892, is in the Campo Fosca, near the scene of his attempted murder, and on his direct way between his cloistered home and the Ducal Palace. The Greatest of the Venetians stands, in monumental bronze, with his face to the street and his back to the canal, and in figure as well as in features he suggests in many ways the younger, and the greater, of the D'Israelis, with whom, except in nationality, he had so little in common.

The D'Israelis, it will be remembered, were descended from a line of prosperous Jewish merchants who had lived here in the days when Venice was still, in a measure,

A CHARACTERISTIC CANAL

the Queen of the Adriatic. Neither of the two men of the race who made it famous in the annals of literature was born here, but they were both of them visitors here, although neither of them has left any record as to where or when. Isaac D'Israeli, however, in a paper upon "Venice," among his *Curiosities*, in refuting Byron's statement that "In Venice Tasso's Echoes are no more," takes bodily and literally, without credit, Goethe's description of how he "entered a gondola by moonlight. One singer placed himself forwards and the other aft, and then proceeded to S. Giorgio." Then follow, in Goethe's words, D'Israeli's remarks upon the music of the gondoliers, closing, still in Goethe's words, with an experience familiar to all subsequent visitors here: "The sleepy canals, the lofty buildings, the splendor of the moon, the deep shadows of the few gondolas that moved like spirits hither and thither, increased the striking peculiarity of the scene; and amidst all these circumstances it was easy to confess the character of this wonderful harmony."

In another chapter of *The Curiosities*, which is entitled "The Origin of the Newspaper," D'Israeli, stealing, perhaps, from somebody else, tells us that the first expression of Literature in the form of a periodical was made in Venice. It was, he says, a Government organ originally issued once a month; and even long after the invention of printing it appeared in manuscript. It was called *La Gazetta*, he adds, perhaps from "gazzera," a magpie, or chatterer, or more likely from "gazzeta," the small Venetian coin which was its price after it appeared in type. If this fact establishes another Literary Landmark for Venice, let Venice have all the credit of it.

Marino Sanudo, the younger and the greater of that name, was one of the early sons of Venice who found his mother neither nourishing, comforting, nor affectionate. He began to take notes, and to make notes, even as a child, his initial researches having commenced before he was ten years of age. He started his *Diary* when he was about seventeen; fifty-six volumes of it, covering a period of almost as many years, are still in existence, although not in Venice; and the larger portions of them have been printed. Besides these, he published voluminous works, all of them of the greatest value to the student of the history of his native state. Mrs. Oliphant calls him "one of the most gifted and astonishing of historical moles." The height of his aspiration was the gratitude and appreciation of the world, by whom he was entirely forgotten for three centuries or more, until Rawdon Brown rescued his name, and his works, from oblivion, and shamed the Venetians into marking, in a suitable way, the house in which he lived; although there is no record of the grave in which he was laid.

Sanudo's house is still standing on the corner of the Fondamenta and the Ponte del Megio, directly in the rear of, and not far from, the Fondaco dei Turchi. It is plain and substantial, what is called a genteel mansion, and it was a worthy home for a plain and substantial and modest Man of Letters. The tablet is weather-worn and stained, and it looks much older than the days of Rawdon Brown. The inscription, roughly translated, states that "Here dwelt Marino Leonardo F. Sanuto, who, while he well knew the history of the whole universe, still wrote with truth and fidelity of his own country and of his own times. He died here in April, 1536."

According to tradition, says Signor Tassini, when Tasso came to Venice with Alfonso di Ferrara to meet Henry III. of France, he lodged in what is now known as the Fondaco dei Turchi, an Italo-Byzantine structure of the Ninth Century, and one of the oldest secular buildings in the city. It stands on the Grand Canal, on the left as one sails from St. Mark's to the railway-station, and past the Rialto; but it was entirely modernized about a quarter of a century ago, and it now contains the collection of the Museo Civico. There is also a tradition that Tasso, in later years, found refuge in the Palazzo Contarini delle Figure, on the other side of the Grand Canal and on the other side of the Rialto Bridge. It is near to the Mocenigo Palace, once the home of Byron.

BYRON'S PALACE, VENICE

Montaigne arrived in Venice in 1580, and his remarks about the city and its inhabitants three centuries ago are quaint and entertaining. He was somewhat disappointed in the show places, but greatly interested in the people. He recorded that he hired for himself a gondola, which he was entitled to the use of, night and day, for two lire *per diem*, about seventeen sous, as he explained, including the boatman. Provisions here he found as dear as at Paris; but then, in other respects, he considered it the cheapest place in the world to live in, for the train of attendants which one required elsewhere was here altogether useless, everybody going about by himself, which made great saving in clothes; and, moreover, one had no occasion for horses. His stay here was very short. He said of Italy generally that he had never seen a country in which there were so few pretty women. And the inns he found far less convenient than those of France or Germany. The provisions were not half so plentiful, and not nearly so well dressed. The houses, too, in Italy were very inferior; there were no good rooms, and the large windows had no glass or other protection against the weather; the bedrooms were mere cabins, and the beds wretched pallets, running upon casters, with a miserable canopy over them; "and Heaven help him who cannot lie hard!"

Milton was in Venice in the months of April and May, 1639, but the only incident of his stay here which he recorded is that he shipped to England a number of books which he had collected in different parts of Italy; and some of these, we are told, by one who saw them later in the lodging-house in St. Bride's Church-yard, London, were curious and rare, "including a chest or two of choice music-books from the best masters flourishing then in Italy."

Among the volumes which Milton bought and studied in Venice was a history of the town, in Latin, printed by the Elzevirs in 1631. It contains the folding-plates of the Rialto, and of the interior of the Council Chamber of the Doges, which are reproduced here; and the well-preserved copy of the same work, bought behind the Cathedral by

THE RIALTO BRIDGE. AS SHYLOCK KNEW IT

the present chronicler, for a few lire, he highly prizes, as presenting views of the public places of Venice contemporary with *The Merchant of Venice* and *Othello*, and as, perhaps, having passed here through Milton's own hands. It was the latest and most authentic chronicle of its kind when Venice received Milton on the bosoms of her canals.

John Evelyn came to Venice in the month of May, 1645, and, as he put it, as soon as he got ashore his portmanteaus were examined at the Dogana, and then he went to his lodging, which was at honest Signor Rhodomante's, at the Black Eagle, near the Rialto, one of the best quarters of the town. The journey from Rome to Venice, he stated, cost him seven pistoles and thirteen julios. "Two days after, taking a gondola, which is their water-coach," he said, "we rode up and down their canals, which answer to our streets. These vessels are built very long and narrow, having necks and tails of steel, somewhat spreading at the beak, like a fish's tail, and kept so exceedingly polished as to give a great lustre." His first visit was to the Rialto. "It was evening, and the canal where the Noblesse go to take the air, as in our Hyde Park, was full of ladies and gentlemen.... Next day I went to the Exchange, a place like ours, frequented by merchants, but nothing so magnificent.... Hence I passed through the Merceria, one of the most delicious streets in the world for the sweetness of it [!]; and is all the way, on both sides, tapestried, as it were, with cloth of gold, rich damasks and other silks, which the shops expose and hang before their houses from the first floor; ... to this add the perfumes, apothecaries' shops, and the innumerable cages of nightingales, which they keep, that entertain you with their melody from shop to shop, so that shutting your eyes you could imagine yourself in the country, when, indeed, you are in the middle of the sea." Evelyn left Venice at the end of March, 1646.

Ruskin, in *The Stones of Venice*, speaks of "the hostelry of the Black Eagle, with its square door of marble deeply moulded in the outer wall, where we see the shadows of its

ENTRANCE TO THE MERCERIA

pergola of vines resting on an ancient well, with a pointed shield carved on its side." This must not be confounded with Signor Rhodomante's establishment, where Evelyn was entertained two centuries earlier. Evelyn's

Black Eagle, after many inquiries among the oldest residents of its neighborhood, and after much interesting and fluent interchange of bad Italian and worse English, was discovered to be the ancient house near the Rialto Bridge, now numbered 5238 Calle dei Stagneri, on the Ponte della Fava, and close to the Campo S. Bartolommeo, where stands the Goldoni statue. The house has retired to private life, and is, at present, the home of a practising lawyer in good standing.

Ruskin's Black Eagle died an unnatural death in 1880, when a certain unusually narrow street was wiped out of existence, under the direction of a chief magistrate (whose name was Dante di Siego Alighieri), to make way for the broad avenue now known as the Street of the 22d of March. The inn was in a retired corner, but on the line of travel between the larger hotels and the Square of S. Moisè. Not a stone of it seems to be left in Venice now.

Ruskin himself, while preserving and polishing *The Stones of Venice*, was very fond of an old-fashioned modest little inn, called La Calcina, in the Zattere Quarter, on the corner of the Campiello della Calcina and by the bridge of the same name. Ruskin's rooms were over the portico, looking out on the Giudecca Canal, and in fair weather he breakfasted and dined under the shadow of a pergola of vines in the very small garden in the rear of the house.

On the Zattere side of this hostelry, over a little gateway in a passage leading to the garden, is a tablet stating that here died the celebrated poet Apostolo Zeno, in 1750. He was born in Venice, eighty-two years before. He came of an old Venetian family, distinguished in the world of letters. He was a poet, "and the reformer and renovator" of the melodrama in Italy, and he wrote works of a serious as well as of a romantic character. His fine library is now a portion of the Library of St. Mark.

During another visit to Venice Ruskin lived in the house of Rawdon Brown (q. v.); and after Mr. Brown's death he lodged at the Hotel Europa. All this information was gathered from his personal guide, who described him as "a very curious man, who looked at things with his eyes shut," imitating, as he spoke, that half-closed-eyelid gaze of a near-sighted person so familiar to all normally visioned observers.

In what is now called the Casa Brown, a stone's-throw from the Calcina Inn, and in the home of his warm friend and literary executor Mr. Horatio F. Brown, lived and worked, while in Venice, John Addington Symonds, and herefrom he went, in the spring of 1893, to Rome to die. Symonds's apartments were on the lower floor of the house, which stands on the Bridge and Campiello Incurabili, of the Zattere. In the upper story were written Mr. Brown's *Venetian Studies*, *Life on the Lagoons*, *The Venetian Printing Press*, etc.

Rawdon Brown lived and died in the Casa della Vida; S. Marcuolo—the address is taken from one of his own visiting-cards. He occupied the second and third floors of this house, which fronts upon the Grand Canal, nearly opposite the Church of S. Eustachio; and many of his contemporary Men of Letters, besides Ruskin, were here his guests. He bequeathed his apartments and their contents to two faithful old servants.

Mr. Brown was buried, in August, 1883, in the Protestant portion of the Cemetery of S. Michele.

Not far from Brown, in the same grounds, lies Eugene Schuyler, "Statesman, Diplomatist, Traveller, Geographer, Historian, Essayist," who died at the Grand Hotel in Venice in 1890.

G. P. R. James, who died in Venice in 1860, was buried in this same Protestant Cemetery. The tablet over his grave, blackened by time, broken and hardly decipherable, contains the following epitaph, said to have been the composition of Landor: "His merits as a writer are known wherever the English language is, and as a man they rest on the heads of many. A few friends have erected this humble and perishable monument." There is a vague tradition among the older alien residents here that James was not buried at S. Michele at all, but on the Lido, where are a few very ancient stones and monuments marking the graves of foreign visitors to Venice. They are in a state of picturesque and utter dilapidation, moss-covered, broken, and generally undecipherable; and none of them seem to be of later date than the middle of the Eighteenth Century. They are within the ramparts of Forte S. Nicolò, near the powder-magazine, and are only seen by the consent of the military authorities, which is obtained with difficulty. It is said that Byron expressed a wish to leave his bones here, if his soul should be demanded of him in Italy.

Sir Henry Layard lodged at the Hotel di Roma in 1867, when began his connection with the glass-works of Murano.

He did not purchase the Palazzo Cappello, on the Grand Canal, corner of the Rio S. Polo, until 1878. Here he received and entertained nearly all the distinguished visitors to Venice, until the time of his death, which occurred in London in 1894.

Mr. Howells, upon his first arrival in Venice, lodged, for a time, in the house of his predecessor as American Consul, in a little street behind the Square of St. Mark. Then he removed to the Campo S. Bartolommeo, on the Rialto side of the square, and later he lived in the Campo S. Stefano before he began house-keeping in the Casa Falier, a queer little mansion on the right-hand side of the Grand Canal, three doors from the infamous Iron Bridge. The Casa Falier has cage-like, over-hanging windows, one of them figuring as "The Balcony on the Grand Canal," from which he saw, and set down, "sights more gracious and fairy than poets ever dreamed."

His latest house here, in 1864-5, was in the Palazzo Giustiniani dei Vescovi, on the other side of the thoroughfare. It is the middle of three Gothic palaces on the Grand Canal which look towards the Rialto, are next to the Palazzo Foscari, and which, as some one has expressed it, are now a

CASA FALIER, WHERE MR. HOWELLS LIVED

mosaic-mill. Here he received and put upon record the impressions of his *Venetian Life*, which have given so much pleasure to so many readers, in Venice and out of it, and which have told us so many things we want to know about Venice and the Venetians.

Mr. Charles Dudley Warner, during one long and happy summer in Venice, wrote the story of his *Winter on the Nile*. He lived in the Barbaro

Palace, on the Grand Canal, not far from the Falier house of Mr. Howells, on the same side of the stream, but on the other side of the Iron Bridge, and nearly opposite the modern-mosaic-frescoed ancient establishment of Murano-work, which Mr. Howells occupied later. Over the front door of Mr. Warner's house is a great carved head of some ancient worthy, perhaps a Barbaro, perhaps a saint or a god, whose rank or title is to-day unknown. Mr. Warner's writing was done in a little room with a balconied window, on the top floor of the neighboring Palazzo Fosclo.

Of the other later-day historians of Venice, it may be stated that Dr. Robertson, the annalist of Sarpi and of St. Mark's, lives in the Casa S. Leonardo, on the Rio S. Maria della Salute, and by the side of the church of that name; that Mr. Augustus J. C. Hare took most of his *Walks in Venice* from the Hotel Milano, fronting on the Grand Canal; that Mrs. Clara Erskine Clement designed her crown for *The Queen of the Adriatic* at the Hotel Europa; and that Mrs. Oliphant made *The Makers of Venice* in a house in the Campo S. Maurizio.

To go back to the men of other days. Addison came to Venice in the winter of 1699-1700. His remarks upon Italy are entertaining enough, although of the guide-book order, and he is uniformly silent regarding his experiences here. As Walpole said of him, he travelled through the poets and not through Italy; all his ideas were borrowed from the descriptions, not from the reality, and he saw places as they had been, not as they were.

Goldoni is one of the few native actors of Venice who merit an encore here. He is as interesting to-day as he was to the audiences who crowded the theatres of Venice to

GOLDONI'S STAIRCASE

witness his performances. He seems to have been born in the Calle dei Nomboli, at the corner of the Ponte and the Fondamenta S. Tomà, in the fine old house which contains the medallion portrait of the poet, and an inscription stating that here Carlo Goldoni first saw the light in 1707. It is still known as the Palazzo Centani, and it still possesses a beautiful Gothic staircase, upon the railing of which a little marble lion still placidly sits. But, as Mr. Howells points out, notwithstanding the assertions of the guides and the guide-books to the contrary, the dramatist could hardly have written many of his immortal comedies here, unless he was unusually precocious even for a poet, for he was a small child when his family moved to Chioggia.

Signor Tassini says that Goldoni was once a resident in the Campo Rusolo, called also Campo Canova. The modern statue to Goldoni, 1883, with its harmonious base, stands in the Campo S. Bartolommeo, near the Rialto Bridge. And there is a tradition that Goldoni was at one time in some way associated with the present Teatro Minerva in the Calle del Teatro S. Moisè, off the modernized Via 22 Marzo, and now the home of the intellectual Marionettes.

In an elaborate and very carefully prepared volume, entitled *J. J. Rousseau à Venise, 1743-1744*, written by M. Victor Ceresole, and published in Geneva and in Paris in 1885, the writer proves very conclusively that Rousseau did not remain so long in Venice as Rousseau declared he did in the *Confessions*; and he points out, upon contemporaneous documentary evidence, that Rousseau occupied the tall thin house in the Canareggio Quarter, which is to-day on the Fondamenta delle Penitente, and bears the number 968. It is the warehouse of a firm of wood merchants, who have removed the grand staircase and have utilized a greater part of the aristocratic old mansion, which was once the home of a powerful Venetian family, and later of the Spanish Ambassadors, as a storehouse for their merchandise, imported from the mountains of Cadore, the land of Titian, and retailed by the innkeepers

GOLDONI'S STATUE

of the present at seventy cents an armful. Rousseau lived long enough in Venice to have added to his own innate power of invention some of the Venetian love of exaggeration; and if, in his *Confessions*, he increased the length of his stay here by at least one-third, it is not easy to say how much of what he said he did here is fiction or fact.

Upon the Ramo dei Fuseri side of the Hotel Victoria and upon the little bridge of the same name is a tablet bearing the following inscription: "*Goethe wohnte hier 28 Sep.-14 Oct. MDCCLXXXVI.*" Notwithstanding the bad reputation for veracity which the Venetian tablets generally have achieved for themselves, and despite the extraordinarily free and phonetic translation of a distinguished American artist from Hartford, Connecticut, to the effect that Goethe "weren't here," it seems from his own confessions that Goethe *was* here, on this identical spot, and at that particular period of his existence, for he wrote: "I am comfortably housed in 'The Queen of England' [so named in honor of the consort of George III.], not far from St. Mark's Square, and this is the greatest advantage of my quarters. My windows look out on a small canal between high houses; directly under me is an arched bridge, and opposite a densely populated alley. So live I, and so shall I for some time remain, until my packet is ready for Germany, and until I have had a surfeit of the pictures of the city. The loneliness I have sighed for with such passionate longing I now enjoy. I know perhaps only one man in Venice, and I am not likely to meet him in some time."

How much Goethe did for Venice, and for the Hotel of the English Queen, Goethe himself probably never knew. But ever since Goethe expressed, in print, his romantic love for the place, German brides have been coming here on their wedding-trips, and have been trying to see Venice as Goethe saw it, and have been quoting Goethe to their husbands-of-a-day-or-two, and have been pretending an enthusiasm for Venice which they do not always feel, simply because, somehow, this is considered, on Goethe's account, the proper thing for German brides to do.

The biographers of Samuel Rogers have printed only fragmentary portions of the *Diary and Letters* written during his visit to Italy in 1814, and very few of his personal experiences here have been preserved. We learn that Venice greatly delighted him, and that he was particularly fond of loitering about the Square of St. Mark. No doubt he was wont to break his fast at the Restaurant Quadri, and very likely he was accustomed to break the fast of the doves who loitered there too.

Byron spent the winter of 1816-'17 in Venice. On the 17th of November, 1816, he wrote to Moore: "I have fallen in love, which, next to falling into the canal (which would be of no use, as I can swim), is the best, or the worst, thing I could do. I have got some extremely good apartments in the house of a Merchant of Venice, who is a good deal occupied with business, and has a wife in her twenty-second year." He spoke more than once of these lodgings, but he gave no hint as to where they were, and he asked Murray to address him *Poste Restante*. Moore, however, says that for many months he continued to occupy the same rooms "in an extremely narrow street, called the Spezzeria, at the house of a linen-draper."

The Spezzeria is not a street, but a district of the town, near the Rialto Quarter. It was devoted, in Byron's day, to the dealers in spices. His Merchant of Venice, therefore, should have been a vender of drugs, sugars, coffees, spices, wax-candles and the like, in wholesale. But, alas for the romance of it all! tradition, in Venice, says that he was a plain, commonplace baker who lived, in good enough style, not in the Spezzeria, but in the Frezzeria, the Street of the Makers of Arrows.

In December Byron wrote to Murray: "I have begun, and am proceeding in, a study of the Armenian language, which I acquire, as well as I can, at the Armenian Convent here, where I go every day to take lessons of a learnèd friar, and have gained some singular and not useless information

BYRON'S STUDY IN THE ARMENIAN MONASTERY

with regard to the literature and customs of that Oriental people. They have an establishment here—a church and convent of ninety monks, very learned and accomplished men, some of them. They have also a press, and make great efforts for the enlightening of their nation. I find the language (which is twin, the literal and the vulgar) difficult, but not invincible (at least I hope not). I shall go on. I found it necessary to twist my mind 'round some severe study; and this, as being the hardest I could devise here, will be a file for the serpent."

He twisted his mind around the Armenian tongue for upwards of half a year, a long time for Byron; and his memory is still held dear among the Armenian brothers, although, of course, none of those are left now who remember him personally; and there are only a few relics of him to be found here. A poor portrait, not contemporaneous; his desk; his inkstand; his pen; and some of his manuscript Armenian exercises are reverently preserved. An aged monk who came to Venice after Byron's day showed me, one sunny afternoon, his own apartment, which he said had once been the English poet's. Although large and comfortable, and scrupulously clean, it is scantily and plainly furnished, and is not very inviting in itself. It has but one window, which is almost directly over the main entrance of the establishment, with an outlook on to the little canal and the open waters beyond. The beautiful old monastery, with its more beautiful old garden, is peaceful and restful; far from the madding crowd, and surrounded by an air of intellect and learning which might tempt one to try to twist one's mind around something sweet and nourishing for one's own sake, if not for Byron's.

On the 14th June, 1817, Byron wrote to Murray again, this time from "the banks of the Brenta, a few miles from Venice, where I have colonized for six months to come." He was again in Venice in 1818 and 1819, and he wrote, "I transport my horse to the Lido bordering the Adriatic (where the fort is), so that I get a gallop of some miles daily along the strip of beach which reaches to Malamocco." At this period he was occupying the centre of the three Mocenigo Palaces, on the Grand Canal.

Moore met Byron in Venice in 1819, and he describes the five or six days they spent together here. He found Byron with whiskers, and fuller both in face and person than when he had seen him last, and leading anything but a reputable life. In Venice portions of *Manfred*, *Childe Harold*, and *Don Juan* were written.

Bakers and poets, in Venice, seem to have a mutual attraction, for there are men still living here who remember Gautier when he was a lodger over the baker's shop in the Campo S. Moisè, on the left-hand side, and opposite the corner of the church, as one goes towards the Square of St. Mark. His landlord, like Byron's, was a Merchant of Venice in bread and cakes, in a retail way; and the establishment is still to be seen on the same spot, its window filled with the staff of life of all sizes and in every shape, some of the latter often fantastic.

The gondolas of Venice have frequently been compared to hearses, but Shelley likened them to "moths, of which a coffin might have been the chrysalis." Clara Shelley, a daughter of the poet, died "at an inn" in Venice in 1818, and "she sleeps on bleak Lido, near Venetian seas."

In *Julian and Maddalo*, written in 1818, Shelley tells us how he—

" ... rode one evening with Count Maddalo
Upon the bank of sand which breaks the flow
Of Adria towards Venice: a bare strand
Of hillocks, heaped from ever-shifting sand,
Matted with thistles and amphibious weeds,
Such as from earth's embrace the salt ooze breeds,
Is this; an uninhabited sea-side,
Which the lone fisher, when his nets are dried,
Abandons; and no other object breaks
The waste, but one dwarf tree and some few stakes,
Broken and unrepaired, and the tide makes
A narrow space of level sand thereon,
Where 'twas our wont to ride while day went down.
This ride was my delight."

The Lido, of course, is here referred to. Later, in the same poem, he says:

"Servants announced the gondola, and we
Through the fast-falling rain and high-wrought sea
Sailed to the island where the mad-house stands."

Elsewhere he speaks of "ocean's nurseling, Venice"; but he never states where he lodged in Venice during any of his brief visits here.

Scott arrived in Venice on the 19th of May, 1832, and he remained here until the 23d. His biographer says that he showed no curiosity about anything but the Bridge of Sighs and the adjoining dungeons, down into which latter he would scramble, though the exertion was exceedingly painful to him. It is not recorded where he lodged here, and he went slowly and sadly home to die.

George Sand and Alfred de Musset spent a number of months, in 1833-34, at the Hotel Danieli, and there De Musset was very ill of a brain-fever, caused, according to the story of old residents, by Mme. Dudevant's desertion of him, although other, and perhaps better, authorities declare that she never left his bedside until he was pronounced out of danger. All statements agree, however, that she was not with him when his brother came for him, in the spring of 1834, and carried him back to Paris.

James Fenimore Cooper, on his arrival here in 1838, "spent a day or two at the Hotel Leone Bianco, on the northwest side of the Square"; but later he "took apartments near the Palazzo, where he set up his own gondola." He did what we all do on our first visit to Venice; but his conclusions are so unlike those of most of us that they are worth recording.

"Although Venice was attractive at first," he says, "in the absence of acquaintances it became monotonous and wearying. A town in which the sound of wheels and hoofs is never known, in which the stillness of the narrow, ravine-like canals is seldom broken, unless by the fall of an oar or the cry of a gondolier, fatigues one by its unceasing calm. I do not remember to have been so much struck with any place on entering it. I do not recollect ever to have been so soon tired of a residence in a capital."

The very absence of the noise of hoof and wheel, the very silence of which he complains, are, to most tired-minded travellers, the greatest of the charms of the capital city of Venice. But happily we each have our own points of view.

Dickens came first to Venice in 1844, when he wrote to Forster: "Here I sit in the sober solitude of a famous inn, with the great bell of St. Mark ringing twelve at my elbow; with three arched windows in my room (two stones high) looking down upon the Grand Canal, and away, beyond, to where the sun went down to-night in a blaze." He did not tell the name of the famous inn; but it sounds like Hotel Danieli. Elsewhere he said to the same correspondent: "My Dear Fellow—Nothing in the world that you have ever heard of Venice is equal to the magnificent and stupendous reality; the wildest visions of *The Arabian Nights* are nothing to the Piazza of St. Mark, and the first impression of the inside of the Church. The gorgeous and wonderful reality of Venice is beyond the fancy of the wildest dreamer. Opium couldn't build such a place, and enchantment couldn't shadow it forth in vision." In 1853 he wrote to Forster: "We live in the same house I lived in nine years ago, and have the same sitting-room—close to the Bridge of Sighs and the Palace of the Doges. The room is at the corner of the house, and there is a narrow street of water running round the side." Again, no doubt, Hotel Danieli.

In 1845 Mrs. Jameson wrote to Catharine Sedgwick: "Did you visit Venice? I forget. In the world there is nothing like it. It seems to me that we can find a similitude for everything else, but Venice is like nothing else—Venice the beautiful, the wonderful. I had seen it before, but it was as new to me as if unbeheld; and every morning when I arose I was still in the same state of wonder and enchantment." She made several visits to Venice, but she gave no hint as to her places of lodgement here.

George Eliot and Lewes arrived in Venice on the night of the 4th June, 1860. "What stillness!" she wrote, "what beauty! Looking out from the high windows of our hotel, I

THE "NOAH CORNER" OF THE DOGE'S PALACE

felt it was a pity to go to bed. Venice was more beautiful than romance had feigned."

On the 15th May, 1864, she wrote to the Trollopes, from the Hôtel de Ville: "We reached Venice three days ago, and have the delight of finding everything more beautiful than it was to us four years ago." Her last visit to Venice was made with Mr. Cross, in the summer of 1880, when her husband was very ill at the Hotel Europa.

Nearly opposite the Europa, on the Grand Canal, stands the Casa Simitecolo, in the parish of S. Gregorio, where Miss Constance Fenimore Woolson died, on the 24th January, 1894. She had, during the preceding year, occupied apartments in the Casa Biondetti, on the same side of the Canal, but nearer the Suspension-Bridge. As was her own desire, Miss Woolson was buried in the Protestant Cemetery in Rome.

Mr. Hare says that Châteaubriand was once a guest at the Europa; and that Wagner, in the same house, wrote a certain Literary-Musical Landmark, called *Tristram and Isolde.* Wagner died in 1883, in the Palazzo Vendramin

Calerghi, on the Grand Canal, a fine mansion, dating back to the end of the Fifteenth Century. It is opposite the Museo Civico, and is sometimes called the "*Non Nobis* Palace," because of the inscription "*Non Nobis Domine, Non Nobis*," in great letters across its front.

In the month of May, 1869, Helen Hunt wrote: "We are most comfortably established at the Hotel Vittoria, *not* on the Grand Canal, thank Heaven! When N—— at first said that she did not dare to stay on the Grand Canal, because she feared too much sea air, I was quite dismayed. But now I am thankful enough to have dry land, that is, a stone floor laid on piles, on *one* side of our house. I look down from any window into one of the cracks called streets; the people look as if they were being threaded into the Scriptural needle's eye, and a hand-organ looks like a barricade." "Cracks called streets" is good.

On "Thanksgiving Day, 1873," Lowell wrote to Thomas Hughes: "To-day the weather is triumphant, and my views of life consequently more cheerful. It is so warm that we are going out presently in the gondola, to take up a few dropped stitches. Venice, after all, is incomparable, and during this visit I have penetrated into little slits of streets in every direction on foot. The canals only give one a visiting acquaintance. The *calli* make you an intimate of the household."

In October, 1881, Lowell wrote to Mr. Gilder from Hotel Danieli: "It is raining; never mind, I am in Venice. Sirocco is doing his worst; I defy him, I am in Venice. I am horribly done; but what can I expect? I am in Venice."

Lord Houghton was living in 1878 at the Pension Suisse, or Hôtel de Rome, on the Grand Canal.

In 1878 Browning was at the Albergo dell' Universo, the Palazzo Brandolin-Rota, on the shady side of the Grand Canal, just below the Accademia and the Suspension-Bridge. Here he remained for a fortnight; and he visited the same hotel again in 1879, 1880, and 1881. In 1885 he occupied a suite of rooms in the Palazzo Alvise, on the other side of the Grand Canal, and about midway between the Grand Hotel and the Hôtel Grande Bretagne; and during the same year he entered into negotiations for the purchase of the Palazzo Montecuccoli, next door to the Albergo dell' Universo, which he used to frequent. He wrote: "It is situated on the Grand Canal, and is described by Ruskin—to give no other authority—as 'a perfect and only rich example of Byzantine Renaissance: its warm yellow marbles are magnificent.' And again, 'an exquisite example [of Byzantine Renaissance] as applied to domestic architecture.' So testifies *The Stones of Venice*." He never owned the palace, however, the foundations of the house proving insecure.

During the last year of his life he lived in a beautifully restored palace on the Grand Canal. It is one of the finest private residences in Europe; but as it is now the home of the poet's son, it is not, of course, except in his absence, open to the public view. It contains many original portraits of Robert and Elizabeth Barrett Browning, by different

THE HOUSE IN WHICH BROWNING DIED

artists and at different ages, a number of bronze and marble busts of them by the present occupant, and notably their private libraries. Never was seen such a collection of absolutely invaluable "presentation copies" from all the writers of note who were the contemporaries and the friends of the wonderfully gifted husband and wife. To at least one visitor to Venice it is the most interesting spot in the interesting city; and he would rather be the possessor of that private library than of all the rest of the great treasures of Venice put together.

Off the library, and on what, for want of a better term, may be called the drawing-room floor, is a bow-windowed recess delicately and exquisitely decorated in white and gold. It was originally the private chapel of that member of the Rezzonico family who became Pope Clement XIII.; and, carefully restored, it has been dedicated by the husband and the son to the memory of Mrs. Browning. It is plainly visible from the larger and the smaller canal; but it was not intended for the world to see, and what is its nature, and what its contents, I have no right yet, and no wish here, to disclose.

On the side of the Browning Palace, above the little Canal of S. Barnaba, and immediately below the windows of the poet's bedroom, is a tablet with this inscription,

"Robert Browning died in this house 12th December, 1889.

"Open my heart and you will see
Graved inside of it 'Italy.'"

This Rezzonico Palace was purchased by Mrs. Robert Barrett Browning in 1888, and here at the close of the next year the poet died. He had said to Miss Browning, not very long before, that he wished to be buried wherever he might chance to breathe his last: if in England, by the side of his mother; if in France, by the side of his father; if in Italy, by the side of his wife. Further interments having been prohibited in the English Cemetery in Florence, where lies his wife, his body was placed temporarily in the chapel of the Mortuary Island of S. Michele here. A few days later he was laid at rest in the Poets' Corner at Westminster Abbey, with "Italy" graved inside his heart.

CPSIA information can be obtained
at www.ICGtesting.com
Printed in the USA
LVHW032034310323
743149LV00006B/968

9 789356 890916